Good For Me
Milk and Cheese

Sally Hewitt

WAYLAND

Notes for Teachers and Parents

Good for Me is a series of books that looks at ways of helping children to develop a positive approach to eating. You can use the books to help children make healthy choices about what they eat and drink as an important part of a healthy lifestyle.

Look for milk and cheese when you go shopping.
- Look at the different types of milk and cheese in your local supermarket.
- Read the ingredients on packets to see if the food contains milk and cheese.
- Buy something new. Have fun preparing it and eating it with children.

Talk about different food groups and how we need to eat a variety of food from each group every day.
- Milk and cheese are packed with vitamins and minerals.
- Talk about the ways vitamins and minerals help to keep us strong and healthy.

Talk about how we feel when we are healthy and the things we can do to help us to stay healthy.
- Eat food that is good for us.
- Drink plenty of water.
- Enjoy fresh air and exercise.
- Sleep well.

First published in 2007 by Wayland
Copyright © Wayland 2007
Wayland
338 Euston Road
London NW1 3BH

Wayland Australia
Hachette Children's Books
Level 17/207 Kent Street
Sydney NSW 2000

Produced by Tall Tree Ltd
Editor: Jon Richards
Designer: Ben Ruocco
Consultant: Sally Peters

British Library Cataloguing in Publication Data
Hewitt, Sally, 1949–
  Milk & cheese. – (Good for me)
  1. Dairy products – Juvenile literature 2. Dairy products
  in human nutrition – Juvenile literature 3. Health –
  Juvenile literature
  I. Title
  641.3'71

  ISBN-13: 9780750250016

Printed in China
Wayland is a division of Hachette Children's Books.

Picture credits:
Cover top Alamy/Photo Network, bottom Dreamstime.com/Edyta Pawlowska, 1 and 9 Alamy/Huw Jones, 4 Dreamstime.com/Jay Schulz, 5 Dreamstime.com/Olga Lyubkina, 6 Dreamstime.com/Jan De Wild, 7 Dreamstime.com/Anneke Schram, 8 Alamy/Agripicture Images, 10 Dreamstime.com/Edyta Linek, 11 Dreamstime.com/Carole Gomez, 12 Corbis/Phil Schermeister, 13 Dreamstime.com/Gordana Sermek, 14 Corbis/A. Inden/zefa, 15 Dreamstime.com/Monika Adamczyk, 16 Rex Features/Phanie Agency, 17 Corbis, 18 Dreamstime.com/Masha Telepneva, 19 Dreamstime.com/Galina Barskaya, 20 middle Dreamstime.com/Christine Mercer, bottom left Dreamstime.com/Sarah Louise Johnson, bottom middle Dreamstime.com/Edyta Pawlowska, bottom right Dreamstime.com, 21 top middle Dreamstime.com/Edyta Pawlowska, centre left Dreamstime.com/Steve Lovegrove, upper centre Alamy/Ingram Publishing, centre right Dreamstime.com/Heath Doman, centre Dreamstime.com/Jack Schiffer, bottom left Dreamstime.com/Rena Schild, bottom middle Dreamstime.com/Joe Gough, bottom right Dreamstime.com/Elena Elisseeva, 23 Alamy/Photo Network

Contents

Good for me

Everyone needs to eat food and drink water to live, grow and be **healthy**. All the food we eat comes from animals and plants. Milk and cheese are food from animals.

Most of the milk we drink comes from cows. Sheep and goats give us milk too.

Milk, cheese, cream and yogurt are all known as dairy foods.

Cheese, cream, yogurt and butter are all made from milk. Milk and cheese are delicious to drink and eat. They are good for you!

Protein

Milk and cheese are a kind of food called **protein**. Protein helps you to grow and gives you energy. Milk and cheese are also full of **vitamins** and **minerals** that give you healthy eyes, skin and hair.

Baby calves drink milk from their mothers because they need protein to grow.

Milk and cheese contain vitamin D and the mineral calcium. These help you to grow strong bones and teeth.

You can have three portions of dairy food every day, such as a piece of cheese or a glass of milk.

Lunch box

Pack a carton of fresh milk for your lunchtime drink.

Milk

On the farm, cows are **milked** every morning and evening. The fresh milk is kept cold. A tanker collects the milk and takes it to a **dairy**.

A machine takes milk from the cows' **udders**.

Machines at a dairy fill
thousands of bottles and
cartons with milk every day.

At the dairy, the milk is heated
to kill any **germs**. Then the milk
is put into bottles and cartons
and taken to shops.

Lunch box

Ask an adult to mix
a banana with some
milk in a blender to
make a tasty smoothie.

Cream and butter

When milk is left to stand, the thick part of the milk rises to the top. This is the cream. Cream contains a lot of fat.

Some kinds of cream are runny and can be poured onto food. Beating air into cream makes it thicker.

Butter is made by stirring or shaking cream until it becomes thick and yellow.

Butter is used for cooking and spreading on bread.

Lunch box

Try using **crème fraîche** on scones instead of whipped cream for a healthier option.

Cheese

Cheese is made by warming up milk. A substance called **rennet** is added to turn the warm milk into thick **curd**. Curd is made into soft cheese such as cream cheese, cottage cheese and ricotta.

As the curd forms, it leaves behind a watery liquid called **whey**.

Hard cheese takes longer to make.
The curd is squeezed and left to dry.
Some cheeses, such as stilton,
contain **mould** which adds blue
specks to them and gives them
a strong flavour.

This girl is eating
a piece of cheddar
which is a kind of
hard cheese.

Lunch box

Try different hard
and soft cheeses in
your lunch box.

13

Yogurt

Yogurt is made from milk and friendly **bacteria** that are good for us. To make yogurt, milk is heated up and the bacteria are added. The milk is cooled down slowly.

As the milk cools, it sets to form thick yogurt that can be flavoured with fruit or honey.

Yogurt mixed with milk
and fruit makes a healthy
fruit smoothie.

Yogurt is sometimes stirred
into stews and soups. Yogurt
with mint, cucumber, lemon
juice and garlic makes a dip
called tzatziki.

Lunch box

Make a sandwich with
flat bread, falafels and
home-made tzatziki.

Buying and storing

Milk, soft cheese, cream and yogurt need to be kept cold to stay fresh. Shops and supermarkets keep them inside large chiller cabinets to keep them fresh.

Dairy foods are printed with a sell-by date, so you can check if they are still good to eat or drink.

Milk will stay fresh
in a fridge for
about a week.

Lunch box

A thermos flask keeps
things cold. Put milk in
a thermos flask to keep
it cold until lunchtime.

Dairy foods soon start to go
bad if they are left in a warm
place. Put them in the fridge as
soon as you can.

17

Cooking milk and cheese

Milk is used to make sauces, soups and puddings. It can be mixed with flour and eggs to create pancake mix. This is poured into a hot pan to make pancakes.

Pancakes can be eaten with sweet foods, such as jam, or savoury foods, such as cheese.

Cooking cheese melts it and makes it soft and runny. Melted cheese can be cooked with cauliflower or pasta to make a healthy meal.

Pizzas are topped with melted cheese and tomato sauce.

Food chart

Here are some examples of food and drink that can be made using three types of dairy food. Have you tried any of these?

Milk

Bowl of cereal   Milkshake   Custard

Cheese

Pizza

Baked potato
with cheese

Pasta bake

Butter

Birthday cake

Garlic bread

Pancakes

A balanced diet

This chart shows you how much you can eat of each food group. The larger the area on the chart, the more of that food group you can eat. For example, you can eat a lot of fruit and vegetables, but only a little oil and sweets. Drink plenty of water every day, too.

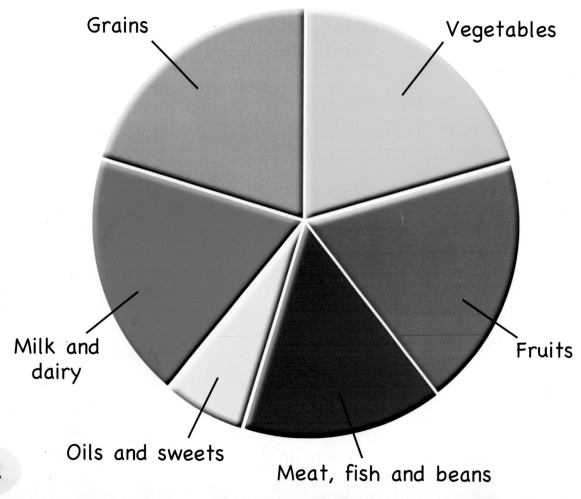

Grains

Vegetables

Milk and dairy

Fruits

Oils and sweets

Meat, fish and beans

Our bodies also need exercise to stay healthy. You should spend at least 20 minutes exercising every day so that your body stays fit and healthy.

Swimming is a great form of exercise that uses muscles all over your body.

Glossary

Bacteria Tiny creatures that can be good for you.

Crème fraîche A type of cream with a slightly sour taste.

Curd A thick substance formed when rennet is added to milk.

Dairy A building where milk is bottled.

Germs Tiny creatures that can be harmful and can make you ill.

Healthy When you are fit and not ill.

Minerals Important substances in food. Calcium is a mineral that helps to build strong bones.

Mould A fungus that is found in some cheeses.

Protein A type of food that helps you to grow.

Rennet A substance that is added to milk to turn it into cheese.

Vitamins Substances that help our bodies stay healthy.

Whey A watery liquid left behind when rennet is added to milk.

Index